with the
Patience
of
Monuments

Poems: Jack Henry

NeoPoiesis Press, LLC

NeoPoiesis Press
P.O. Box 38037
Houston, Texas 77238-8037

www.neopoiesispress.com

With the Patience of Monuments, by Jack Henry
ISBN 10 0-981-99842-9 (paperback : alk. paper)
    1. Poetry. I. Henry, Jack II. Kenney, Thomas

Printed in the United States of America.

First Edition

some of these poems have appeared previously and i wish to thank those editors for their generosity:

erbacce press; shoots and vines; children, churches and daddies; deep tissue magazine; kill poet; epic rites; word slaw; new aesthetic; mad swirl; oak bend review; off beat pulp; lit up magazine; cause & effect magazine and scintillating press

and

kendra steiner editions *for permission to reprint portions of "empty houses," and* **erbacce press** *for permission to reprint portions of "the downtown café."*

Also by *Jack Henry*

Scrawl (K3 Press, 2006)
Chasing Screaming Monkeys
    Without Any Clothes (d/e/a/d/b/e/a/t press, 2007)
Snow in Summer and the Playground
    is Closed (scars publications, 2008)
The Downtown Café (erbacce press, 2008)
Empty Houses (kendra steiner editions, 2009)

for kelly, as always

&

*my mother and father,
who support me no matter what
name i go by*

&

*breana,
who reminds me that
things accepted
are sometimes amazing*

&

*lacey,
who reminds me that
youth is not always
wasted on the young*

Contents

when *Dale Winslow* asked me if i wanted to do a full length book of poetry i hesitated. anyone that publishes poetry, large or small, wants to make some profit and i couldn't imagine anyone wanting to buy my book. and don't think i am being humble. i am a huge narcissist with a gigantic ego and an over-inflated sense of self-worth.

i only hesitated a second.

for a few months i gathered, collated, folded and stapled together a manuscript of poems i thought would be of some interest, poems filled with sex, drugs, death and dying. a sort of anti-poetry homage. she had asked for poems that had a thread, a theme, a link and i just laughed. i remember laughing. it scared the cat.

one Sunday she called me and said she found a theme. i started to laugh again. she said, *you have a religious theme to your poetry.* i hung up the phone.

immediately i reread everything i sent. to my shock and utter dismay, i had written religious tinged poetry, but religious in a way that won't assist my efforts to gain entrance into either *Heaven* or *Hell.*

we spoke again, after i promised not to hang up, and agreed, reluctantly, to her summation. we settled on the term *religiosity* and *spirituality.* the thought that i write religious anything makes me want to snort chalk dust until my brain bleeds.

at this point you might as well buy it. if you don't like it donate it to your local church book sale. then it's a tax write off and i can piss off another priest.

jck hnry
toad suck, ca
june 2009

Em or F# on a slide trombone

a single note destroyed me,
as easily as *Hitler* destroyed *Europe*,
in those echoes we
sometimes refer to
when other metaphors feel too tame

so-called trust and faith,
a metronome time click -
i failed to see humor
in your monotone reply –

it didn't seem that hard when
you finally hit [send]

robbed of my passion, my desire
these games i play, pity party
party of one – i want nothing
more to do with it

i roll from the counter
with my cocaine curfew
dispassionate rhythms
of a jazz infused cry

very next breath

look, i'm no *Ezra Pound*
not that it was an ambition
although i like the name *Ezra*
but that's not the point

i am more like a sea monkey
in a jar of *Vaseline*
set upon a shelf
with a dusty lid
next to a peeling dildo
the one that hasn't touched
hot flesh in fifteen years

or maybe
i am like a rollercoaster
you know, the wooden kind
used to live large and bright
and shiny on an East Coast pike
but now splintered
filled with termites
crickets and armies of rabid mice

some might suggest
i am an old book
stuck on a library shelf,
misplaced behind philosophy texts
or encyclopedias,
the kind of library
that has every
other light turned off
because they can't pay the bill,
the kind of library where
people volunteer
out of boredom
and general decay

perhaps i'm like *Jesus*,
during those middle years
no one writes about,
from books the church decided
were best left unread, because
i think *Jesus* did shit no one wants to remember,

most likely i am *none of the above*,
a long blank page slightly yellowed
from too much sun,
an old tire in a weed infused field,
a rotting apple beneath the dust of a dying tree,
a child in a *Cambodian* orphanage just
after *Angelina Jolie* added to her collection

there's a chance i am just a mirror,
broken on the floor in a symphony of silver shards,
awaiting the dust pan and a trip to the curb

in the end it doesn't matter,
because once i discover who i am,
it changes with the
very next breath,
and the next breath
carries the rattle of a dying man

mouse but not Mickey

i feel like a mouse
without other mice
to torment me
only cats
gray and black and white
but we talk a little
about cheese
and wine
and sunsets over *Palm Springs*

we talk about
Voltaire
Hemingway
and *Frank O'Hara*

these cats seem to know
more than a mouse might
they listen
i am deaf
the ringing in my ear
reminds me of night bombing
in *Laos*
or, perhaps, a blizzard
in the *Arctic* or, even better,
rice being thrown at
a wedding

they huddle in herds
gaggles or groups,
it's not a murder of cats
that i do know
but i am just a mouse
with broken feet
and bad ears
although i have a good tail
that's easily bust

when the sun gets
too close, as it sometimes can,
i race for the black recess
of tortured rocks
the cats can't see me hear me

but i watch

they dance and sing
the way cats sometimes do,
i hear their harmony
and sweet voices

i ate a bug because
i couldn't find the cheese
and sometimes, when
you're hungry
you'll eat anything that moves

N'orleans mornings

N'orleans mornings
sky gray to blue
footsteps scrape across
cobblestone roads
past dead gates
flat stone memories
echoes sound
bubble pop exclamation

she's alive in life

flood tides break
levee walls call me
back to sandstone
etchings atop glass
houses where ghosts
play cards and remember
through trees whispering
on forgotten wind

Spanish moss plays
gentle tricks
on my thoughts
you, me, velvet kisses
stolen before gargoyle
eyes where my hand rests
gentle upon supple curves
linger through moments
incandescent shadows
flicker
through sweet fragrant
tides and pools long
for release to the sea

she's alive and screaming

words seamless fall
sporadic cries ring
tin bell whistle chime
through harbors of steep
castle walls clang light
halyard clank soft atop
silver flat serenade

N'Orleans nights ask
questions unanswered during
phone lines discontent
players dance through
a surrender of souls and
cavalcades of bittersweet
love lost longing i love you
words scattered across lines
where i end wrapped warm

there's a harbor in my heart for the soulless in decline

there's a gray hair at the end of my nose
sometimes i stare at it in the bathroom mirror
right after i tie my shoes and uncap a whiskey bottle

sometimes i stand in the street just before a rainstorm
when life is thick and full of heat, when dreams became
matinees at the old theater

sometimes i drive downtown, order hot pastrami on
wheat because rye bread would remind me of you

sometimes i drive up *Mulholland*, past big homes
with the shiny cars and *Mexican* maids named *Lupita*
and gardeners named *Pete*

   i never lived in a big house, with a garden, a proper garage
   and a purpose beyond existing
   it's just a box where i stay –
   four walls, a roof and a front door
   that squeaks from too much passage

   when i sit on the curb and watch rainwater carry cigarette
   butts to the ocean, where they gather in wastewater basins
   and continue to kill, i listen for the banter of crows and cats,
   demagogues and demons
   there's a harbor in my heart for the soulless in decline

sometimes i take plane rides to cities of no purpose
just stand at the counter, buy passage, next flight out -
one time i sat next a poet who called himself "Thunder"
i just laughed because i had to pee

   there's a tall woman in tight jeans, standing in front of me,
   waiting on a restroom – her smile's *Portuguese* translated to
   Romanian, we dance in the galley, fuck on a commuter bus

she likes to remember each encounter
with a picture and proper blogging
if i didn't know what i was doing,
i'd never make it home by five

shower sputters as heat begins to beg,
i wipe condensation from a mirror,
i pluck that single gray follicle, flick it to the floor

there's a panther in the playground
the blue pill begins to dissolve

sublimation

i am a 1950s suburban housewife standing at the door,
knowing but not wanting him to return after a day at the office
or an afternoon with his whore
alone in the kitchen masturbating to memories, lost in a fog of
anti-depressants and household chores, *Leave it to Beaver*
beatitudes and paint-by-numbers *Barbie* play sets

i am a black man working as a porter in an *Atlanta* hotel, 1963,
listening to a radio, news from *Dallas*, carrying
a white man's bag, waiting for a quarter tip, invisible to all
except a couple's smiling little girl, her mother says, *do not talk
to that man*

i am a homosexual locked in a bar, *New York City*, 1966,
a vice cop's cock in my mouth, handcuffs on my
wrists, boot in my guts, arrested, taken downtown
and put in a cell with 30 other straight men that eye me with
anger and fear and hate

i am *Christ on the Cross*, wind in my hair,
women at my feet, crying and chanting, waiting on the spear of
a *Roman* soldier, watching the sun drift across the sky, waiting
for eternity, wondering if returning might not be an option,
wishing i had taken more time, but knowing that destiny is not
mine,

nor will it be

death before dying

maybe the wind had it right
always move, never linger
never more spiritual than a moment
never a voice without beginning

i sit sheltered and lost
forlorn, a bit, because my words
are in transition and i am disconnected
from its progress

they have taken my walking stick
a talisman from dead poets
and other odd fucks that no longer
ring church bells and add to the
fodder of war torn realities

i am stuck
i am dead
i am drowning
i am inept

death before dying
before mourning
before six feet of dust and sand
before excommunication
from vivid tales of murmur and mirth

within each pause a castle falls
and we sit crushed under lumber and rock
waiting, always waiting
for the mouth of the *Nile* to open

bougainvillea

the pool is filled with drifting leaves
of bougainvillea
i drown in beauty

a bright light dims
it's time to go home
the wind that once told stories
has folded its ambition
the water is warm

days flow by unevenly
dawn to dusk we keep running
i smoke a cigarette and everything begins

i bought dope from an *Aryan* porter
his thick hands and smooth skin
made me smile for a bit

it's funny how quickly i lose
concentration
ideas glisten
thoughts die
what i think is funny
rarely makes her laugh

in the morning
little birds sing with great enthusiasm
i just sigh
frozen exhale
i wake my porter
and send him home

rules to a game

i don't live a *Christ* centered life,
or, wash my feet before i enter a mosque,
or, stay away from pork or caffeine or heroin

i don't cross a street when black teenagers
walk up the same sidewalk as me

i don't avert my eyes when a homeless man
reaches out to me with dirty hands, or,
when a recovering addict asks for donations
in front of a grocery store

i don't work for a chemical company that's
only interested in profits and not the environment,
or a oil company that insists current profits are fair,
or a government that believes torture and war
are resolutions to disagreement

i don't vote because all the candidates are paper plates,
and the point escapes me when they say change
and the only change is the player but the games
remain the same

i don't remember your name, or, keep your picture, or
hold onto memory of false promises, lies, and truths designed
to placate my passion

i don't listen to the radio to hear the news because i
see the news on my street every day, or watch television
because i no longer care if *Britney* flashes her cunt or *Lindsey* is
a lesbian or if *Paris* is going to prison for ten days when the
rest of us get life

i don't love her now that i realized she never loved,
or fuck with passion because i paid too much
or drink when i know the gutter will be my bed

i don't wander aimlessly any more than i normally do,
or, run with friends that see nothing but the moment,
or, chase dreams because cost has become too much

i don't watch others kiss
or, breathe in the perfume of a beautiful woman
or, look at light coming from the eyes of a passing saint or,
wistfully reflect on what could have been

i don't say no when offered the needle
or the pipe, or a fat round joint, or a hand job without
commitment, or a blowjob by a crackwhore

i don't live life like the brochure offered
or live on a street where kings and queens reside
or play like my heart sometimes remembers

i don't tune out the sounds of lovers fucking in the
apartment above me, or masturbate, because the effort
is too much

i don't call the police when a gunshot sounds
and the body drops with an ominous thud,
or when a man in a black ski mask robs a liquor store
at gunpoint, or when a mugger takes my meager funds

i don't listen to gospel music, or rock and roll,
or the blues, especially the blues because that
music rings in my ears 24/7 already

i don't wake up with anyone i know
or want to know, that would just be
the first step toward departure

i don't say nice things when a preacher offers
salvation, or a bartender offers on the house, or
when my last friend needs comfort

i don't know who i am, or who i will be, or
where i am from

i don't walk in crowds, or go to the theater,
or spit on the sidewalk, or piss on the back walls
of a sacred place

i don't remember faces, not since the fire took my own,
not since time wore my bones down with insignificant
precision

i don't go to doctors, the last one's opinion
became a prophesy

i don't write poetry, or sonnets, or joyful
tomes about birds and butterflies, those words
are taken and mean less each time repeated

i don't do anything, especially now, especially
when the devil has your nuts in a silk bag,
especially when your hands commit the unspeakable,
especially when my eyes see nothing but this

if

if i could only write
or dream
or empty the sand
from my vans tennis shoes
the ones with the holes
in the toes
and my soul worn down

if i could only taste
the bitter fruit,
find flavor deep in
the belly of an east coast
castle

i rise each day
tie myself
to the chain
my hands thick on the keys
punching holes
in memories
and telepathic
heart murmurs

nothing seems to stick
falling from the page
ready for the dustpan
random thoughts
scattered with the offal
of a disinterested life

i browse and peruse
wander through the sticky pages
wonder what my next thought
will be but know
before words drool from
my lips

if i could rise above
where i stand, where i scream
my head bloodied
from a tireless pursuit

i shot all the sheep
for fear of the wolf

if i could cross the line
hold her heart, or her hand
if i could speak the truth
perhaps i would
(then again...)

if i could only know
before knowing
see through my blindness

untitled

i have a table
made of old wood
wood from stolen planks
of dying ships

i sit in a red chair
bought at
a thrift store
with money
meant for whiskey
and other essentials

i stab out another
cigarette in the cup
of *Christ* i found
unattended at a local
Catholic Church

i watch the sun
wisp across dirty windows
as the cries of children
thick with life
laugh at the school
across the alley

i write poetry
on scraps of paper
i inherited from
the estate of
an uncle i never knew

i pause
to consider
my standing
in life but grow tired
and nap

i read chapbooks
by warriors
and odd fellows
filled with
brilliant light

i pick scabs
and watch red trails
laze to the floor
with startling splashes

i sit at my table
in my chair
with my paper still blank
in front of me as the sun folds
and night double downs
and whispers become fever and blood
becomes
stale

eulogy for a memory of an idea that never really existed

1.   this will never see light,
        because light
        is a theory
        of existence and sustenance
        of which we are yet to realize

        this will never hold meaning,
        you have fought too hard
        to realize that everything
        is done,
        perhaps
        before you started,
        perhaps
        before you woke up

        this will never become a classic,
        or a charter of truth, or an identifiable beginning
        or end,
        this
        will
        never
        become

2.   to a specific man
        standing
        there standing
        a specific man
        or woman
        building
        monuments
        of straw
        and gum
        building
        small temples
        of sticks

and pie
of dead word
poets
and metaphor
building
and climbing
yes i am
i am
yes
i am i am
building and building
a specific man
or woman
it's you i watch

3.   there is no underground
no battlefield
no war
no battle
no conflict

there is no outside
or inside
no middle
no up
no down and down and down

4.   i no longer bleed
my bloody temple
stapled shut
sharp corners
smoothed down
sanded fine
and slick
wet with molding
pus and the stink
of a rotting cunt

i no longer move
when your words
cry, when your squalor
rises and steals your breath,
when the abyss bridges
front to back and lies
become the fodder
of a morning meal

i no longer slow
when worlds rush past,
collide, fold and deplete
the last remaining smiles
of disconsolate angels

i no longer see
a battlefield, or war,
or conflagration

5.   *(for sa griffin)*
we are born cool
cool and cool
like blue fire cool
born into this
and this
born
cool and cool
modern moments
nothing more
cool and cool and cool
we are born

6.   i am no underground
i am no poet
i am no believer
i am no traveler
i am no dreamer
i am no realist (most days)

i am no existence
i am no preacher
i am no pilot
i am no sky
i am no dance or song or melody in a minor key
i am no light
i am no shadow
i am no front or back
i am no parade
i am no glory
i am no exclamation
i am no pastoral precedence
i am no goal
i am no end
i am no poet
i am no underground,

it never existed

7.   i'm not looking for you to stand with me
or near me
or on my street
i am not looking for a preacher
of the word or hope and life
and some fucking light
at the end of a sewer tunnel

these are all lies you twisted
on your countertop, mixed
with cigarette butts and analogies
your sainted eyes keep looking
down on me DOWN on me
as I look up between your
salted legs, UP and OUT

8.   to the congregation i say:

"we will miss [fill in the name of the decedent]

they offered us hope and joy
they offered us passion and delight
they offered us desire and fulfillment
they offered us present and past

we will miss [fill in the name of the decedent]
because of the joy they brought to all the people
[he/she] touched on a daily basis.

ashes to ashes, dust to dust..."

[insert sound of crying and caskets lowering
into six feet of dirt]

to the mirror i say:

"they never knew, nor understood -
it became an image they could not comprehend -
this is a eulogy for a memory of an idea
that never really existed
and when they awake
we will have to rediscover our
own footsteps and cut our chain
to our bloody string of lies."

to my future i say:

i will start again each day
i will awake and be ready
i will stretch and try
i will never care what another says about me
i will never look back

three lines in

three lines in
and i want to cut off
my arm, beat you to death
with the bloody stump

it's worse than reading
Braille with my dick
at least there i
get a little feeling

perhaps you should
sew your eyes shut
and see through a proper
lens or, maybe, cut off your
fingers and type with your
toes

i keep hearing the grind
grind
grind
of plastic gears
mold back into mush
trite gibberish
any gibbon's monkey
could recite

perhaps if you buried
yourself
into a mound of
red ants you might understand
feeling
or
if you took fiberglass
and licked it with your fat
cow tongue

maybe if you were keelhauled
or drawn n' quartered or tortured
with speeches of *Bush* and *Cheney*
fastened to a chair naked with duct
tape, or fisted by a silverback guerrilla

perhaps then you'd know how
i feel when i get three lines in
and the pus in my eyes begins
to seal them shut

insufficient payment

grass
cool upon
my skin

sky
bright
and holy

trees
eager to please
bend at will
as low winds
draw down
the magnificence
of it all

concrete
hard
beneath my shoes
as i walk careless
carefree
and alive

the day
invigorating
life
tremendous

my muse
has emerged
from
her hiding

1.   i walk atop
brown boards
old and creaking
whispered winds
tell me
old friends' passage
water sweeps across
morning tide
you were there
sweet as summer
finding clouds drifting
from simple tides
little crabs clamber
jetty rocks statuaries

i walk atop
creaking embers
each step a triumph
i move through
basking in glory
midday sun
boats on the bay
gentle glide across sullen seas
old friend not forgotten
words shared
echoes in lamplight
clanging halyards

i walk atop a stone wall
sun in my hair
wind in my teeth
watch for the setting
you are gone
lost in a tangle of blue-red memory
gone from present
buried in no past

2. thirty-six years now
    since i last touched
    your smile
    my eyes drift back
    slow in
    recollection
    timid
    in response
    i see you
    your yellow hair
    purple dress
    like *Easter*
    like summer
    life memories scattered
    only to surface when i smell the sand

    that first touch
    a lingering smile
    a first kiss
    tragic as exotic
    that first moment

    lives even now

3. two years ago ages ended, forever began
    you stepped light across a threshold of sand

    we said little, did everything
    words wash away sins of collected pasts
    dark room cooled from a buzzing a/c
    you held onto me, a beautiful gargoyle
    luminescent eyes
    watching, protecting, offering

    your delicate touch destroyed spreading sorrow
    reached in and offered me hope

absolved of nothing, but trying

1.   i watch two old people
with gray hair and rumpled clothes
a bit stooped, delicate in movement

walking

a man and woman
hand in hand like a sentimental
commercial selling wedding
rings and promise

they smile at me as i
pass them by, smile at each other

when they turn a corner
they vanish into light

2.   i sit on the back porch of an old house
filled with memory and dog hair,
filled with joyful mornings
filled with laughter and, recently,
sorrow and pain

absolved of nothing, i burned
her spirit, her pride, the course
of her day – i failed her
failed myself – and those
gathered at her side

i nearly lost
    my beautiful gargoyle
    my perfect poem
    my spectacular life

in a single act, one gunshot
snapping turtle tap dance

almost pissed away an existence
of a thousand memories
an unlimited future

each day i push forward
start again, on bended knee
forgiveness asked

she took me back

it should not have taken fire
to make life so clear
but from ash, life returns

a single chance, a last opportunity
building back to a greater love

3.   i love you
and i will bring meaning
back to those words
i need you,
because life without you
is life without
i cherish and adore you
more than i ever knew

if my eyes ever close they will close
forever, if my heart ever fades it
is because i am dead

each day
i will breathe for your absolution
each day
i will never forget

i want you forever
and nothing more

4.   she walks around the corner
with a particular smile
i know is mine, one
that says you're still an asshole
but i am here completely

i am here
completely
as well

we chat a bit about the day
clouds gather and mingle
slowly fade

i take her hand, kiss her,
make her blush with a particular
whisper, one i have that
is only for her, one that
says i love you, thank you, i promise
i am working on it, continuously

with a steady grip
she leads me
from the back porch
to the bed
we fold together
in a tangle
of linen,
each kiss brings
us closer,
each touch gives me
hope

5.   an old couple sits on the back porch
of an old house filled with laughter
and memory,
and hopeful tomorrows

he brushes strands of gray hair
from her eyes and she smiles

little children scream and laugh
a blended family of dogs and cats
and 20 years of rediscovery

she holds his hand, kisses him
soft on his aging lips, leads
him behind double locked doors
as the fold together in linen

even now, with promises fulfilled,
they rise from ash,
rise from past
sorrow

an old tattoo across her skin
stills says
Jack,
the tattoo on
his shoulder still says i'm sorry

on the verge of an every day tomorrow

she stands on stage
- total control
they eat every word from her giving hands

i watch -
nearly gone
- from sucking down
grain alcohol and tequila
death stands waiting,
i'm long overdue

- her light blinds me
in the black of my day
- her essence crushes
my spine

she's a dark torment i keep in my pocket
- the what if
- the could have been
- the 'i'll never know'

from afar i watch
she grows like a juniper tree,
tall and fast to the sun

and i sit still
as alcohol replaces my blood
and i breathe fire

our eyes connect
at the close of her last line

her eyes
never fall
but mine
can only look away

my eyes brilliant blue

i remember the last time we met
walking through fire
across burning coals
laughing
you were young then
younger than i could ever be
now i lay in chambers of stone
alone on a steel cot

you came to see me
        here i am
behind the iron rod
        here i am

remembering

we used to laugh sometimes
in that cabin up in *Big Bear*
the one without heat
careless, perhaps reckless
always on the run

my feet no longer move that way
twenty years gone
no contact
i fell down a dark hole
a portal of unfathomable longing

you married, had a family, found suburbia
and i criss-crossed the country
seeking what you had discovered

you visited me smart suit
perfect tie
shining shoes
me in my orange jumpsuit

we talked about old days
strange days
experimenting with life
tasting glory
then you left
and here i am

tomorrow is my birthday
no visitation scheduled
i have grey hair
tweaker teeth
down but not broken
my eyes brilliant blue

the guards
know my name
i tell them stories
about you and me
back
when the earth stood still
and everything lay flat

destroyed by hope

i watch the sun rise
through green leaves.
dogs bark, birds sing,
cars race along the road.
my mind races without pause,
neurons snap through fissures
that beg forgiveness when
my fingers caress the rope.

she offered promise,
desire fulfilled, yet the sentence
announced perpetual miscalculation -
i stood before *Christ*
and pushed in the blade.

unbound from my heart,
crows peck at remains -
i drift slow through
vapors of heat rising
from black asphalt -
her smile burns my flesh
as simple as chance
destroys my soul.

a bookstore on Bleecker Street

she had crossed eyes and a slight limp
but i didn't mind when she kissed me good morning
and made me pancakes

we met at a bookstore over on *Bleecker Street* during an
electrical storm in *December*

the owner freaked out, kicked everyone to the curb
the gimp and i sat at a coffeehouse
watched the rain tap *Morse* code

the city emerged when power returned
from its temporary nap,
we held hands
wobbled over to her low rent fifth floor walk-up apartment

she had a one-eyed cat
with a bent tail and *Tourettes* syndrome
that ate tuna from the can and
old artichoke hearts on a chipped plate

she said,
it's been so long since i have had sex, i've forgotten how to do it
later i find out it's an absolute lie

we sat on the floor next to half open window,
drank whiskey from a bottle and listened to for lightning
she said her name was *Alice*, i tell her i am *Jesus* –
i stuck a popsicle in her pussy and
read passages from *Shakespeare's Twelfth Night*

on *Sunday* we went to a cathedral,
ate church in the back row,
sang songs by the *Ramones*
when everybody knelt to pray

i bought her correction shoes
so she would walk normal
she bought me trannie heels
because her roll is a little off

she died that next *Thursday*,
for reasons i was never offered,
the doctors in their pimp suits simply muttered
benignly walked away

i took over the rent at her apartment,
kept everything situated,

the cat sits beside me with tuna on its breath

planes fly here to there and it's really no business
of mine except telegraph landmines set memories
in motion and acid boils to the tips of parched lips

no longer a bag to punch, i will delete pain as easily
as you denied me simple conversation at the gates
of your thorny crown

> **hate**
> *–verb (used with object)*
> 1.   to dislike <u>intensely</u>
> or <u>passionately</u>; feel extreme
> <u>aversion</u> for or extreme
> <u>hostility</u> toward; <u>detest</u>:
>
> - to hate the enemy;
> - to hate bigotry;
> - to hate pervasion

mind fucking that leaves me coiled in corners
surrounded by empty soldiers that no longer
bring comfort, rather contempt, self-loathing

definitions keep sounding, i see them on every page
guaranteed no satisfaction, return is no longer an option

at each turn, disappointment

> **promise**
> *–noun*
> 1.   a <u>declaration</u> that something will
> or will not be done, given, etc., by one:
> - i promise to call you
> - i promise to be honest
> - i promise to respect and acknowledge
> 2.   something that has the effect

of an <u>express assurance</u>; indication
of what may be <u>expected</u>.
–verb (used with object)
3.   to <u>engage</u> or <u>undertake</u> by promise
(usually used with an infinitive or a clause as object)
4.   to make a promise of something
to (<u>a specified person</u>)

i can no longer limp along flaccid, hollow, denied

my expectations too big, my contempt complete

please do not call, my number does not exist
upon further reading you will discover a
perfect rendition of what and who i have become

fool
–*noun*
1.   a silly or stupid person;
a person who <u>lacks judgment</u>
<u>or sense</u>.

asthmatic love songs

i lay on the lip of your last lie
folded into spasms of faded reality
complicated by dead voice screams
mother, the children are dying,
echoes from the television

two flies fuck, neither up or down,
yet, somehow, side to side, flagrantly
tossed by bellow's wind intent on
completion, and i know i'm not like that

yet your visceral delusions bring me
nothing but weak phases and tired
turning of rumored recovery, it's written
here somewhere –

maybe not

i read your bible verse, posted on
a refrigerator door, covering trashcan
advertisements - free tune up, free estimate,
10 dollars off with purchase, but wait there's more

we slide down though a yearning abyss,
tempted by thrust and shove moments,
hesitant to change the channel without a remote
burned in asthmatic love songs

at seven

at seven
my father would take
me to work with him
give me a handful of quarters
and a wad of dirty dollars -
told me i'd be alright
and
to come back
by around 3 o'clock

i would walk up and down
the slippery sad sidewalks
of downtown
Los Angeles
peek into lives
without knowing
which verb
connected a noun

old men
with dusty carts filled
with tin cans
sleeping bags
and
other polluted things
would stare
at me through sloppy eyes
speak
with rheumy lips

every time
i gave them a quarter
they'd tell me a story
like the one
i'm telling now

at noon
i eat lunch
at a deli counter
at the international
marketplace
no one cared if a
little white kid
wanted to buy a meal

Los Angeles never cared about much

at the end of the day
after hunting
through dumpsters
and
dreaming
through red lights
i'd walk back
to my father's work
and
sit
in silence as we drove home

he kept his stories
just like i kept mine

Christ *on the streets of* Los Angeles *in 1977*

when i was 13
i saw *Christ* on the streets of *Los Angeles*
up near *Angel's* flight
and the international food market

he carried spray cans
tagged white walls with
words of sorrow
angst and derision

back then my father smoked more often
cursed in equal numbers
but never saw the same streets
that i did

he gave me three dollars
and a quarter
i bought
watermelon and beef jerky
i sat alone in a park while my dad
talked to god

Christ told me to ignore
the canon
the kind you find in a bookshop

i told him that he forgot
to cross a "t" in *Christmas*

he frowned
and wandered

away

Jesus of Los Angeles, pt 1

Jesus of *Los Angeles*
sits in the corner booth
at the *Speak Easy Tavern*,
turning *LA* tap water into merlot

twelve friends sit together
arguing over baseball
gesturing wildly and
laughing

they are friends,
you can see that
after years of struggle
along skid row

rainy day - late *November*
Tom has a gig
poetry reading
at the *Iconoclast Bookstore*

Jesus doesn't say much
smiles serenely
lets others speak
he watches the *Cubs*

play baseball - day game,
Cubs down - 3 to 1
i sit quietly nearby
saying nothing

my girlfriend
Holly Hollywood
semi-beautiful pre-op transsexual
left for *Florida*
first flight out

family - she says
appearances and such
back in a month
kiss her goodbye with a sigh

i spend my evenings
belly up at the *Speak Easy*
sitting with friends
and strangers

we talk of baseball
and politics - old / new
various related points
of triviality

Big Bill serves cheap beer
reads the sports page
a junkie named *Loretta*
sleeps in the back

and *Jesus* watches baseball
drinks his wine
sits with friends
and laughs

Jesus of Los Angeles, pt. 2

Jesus
   of *Los Angeles*
cheers on his team
Chicago Cubs
baseball

midday game
on the
flickering black and white
at the *Speak Easy Tavern*

a variety of friends
   hangers on - mostly
stay close by his side
waiting for magic
   but not really sure

in between innings
he falls silent
they bury him in questions
but he never speaks

when the game continues
they fall silent
   friends
   and hangers on

each of us
   searches
every day
looking for hope
- a moment
- a promise of something
we never saw
   or
already passed by

at the end of the game
Jesus
  of *Los Angeles*
pays his tab and waves goodbye

no one follows
no one knows the way

for a while they mill about
lost and confused
then drift away
  as well

Jesus
  of *Los Angeles*
slips in the back door
after the friends
  and hangers on depart
takes his meds and swallows
them down with a shot of tequila

his eyes grow heavy
and he loses the robe
leaves it the old coatroom

out the front door
back into the heat of *September*

he trudges up the street
to a half way house
finds his room and waits
for peace

Jesus of Los Angeles, pt. 3

i thought i saw
Jesus
standing at the checkout
of a *99 Cent Store*

he spoke
calmly into
his cell
phone,
waiting his
turn at the
register

no one
else
saw what
i saw

he bought
cans of beans
bag of carrots,
a package
of paper plates
and double "A"
batteries

i got a
text from
Old Scratch
said:
"no waiting
in the next line"

Jesus of Los Angeles, pt. 4

i remember
watching
Jesus of *Los Angeles*
guide traffic
over on *6th* and *LA St*
when the streetlights went
dark

he smiled
and
seemed to be
having a great
time

and i
remember laughing
because it
made no sense
then
and even less
sense

now

prayer and departure

my balls itch
but that's not the point
i live in the box
with my freedom -
soul – and related accouterments
the buzzing of the freeway
only keeps me awake on weekends

we sit next to each other
in the kitchen
on long wooden benches
the preacher says a prayer
but i didn't learn the words
his eyes never seem to leave me
and i understand why

when it's too cold for the street
we curl up on cots
close to each other
and the unique stink we all have

i never hear the screaming
my mind locks it out
and the cotton in my ears
keeps me whole most of the time

every now and then
things turn
and i catch up
i buy a room and a bath
and a razor or two

the hopelessness of wanting
always puts me back to the stone
my feet trace the path
we all cut

migration takes me north
and a different nuance
i find space behind a warehouse
between poet and priest

when the sun greets me
at the beginning of the day
everything seems fine
when the rumble in my gut hits
i begin to question
and when that last craving
burns i pray the light of day
just leaves me alone

with the patience of monuments, i burn

we stand silent
staring down memories
with the patience of monuments
i burn

old stone flesh
chips away
amidst the stains
of an obedient sun

summer feels so far

heat curls from cast iron stoves
widows huddle close
listen to songs of *Christ*
and work crossword puzzles
filled with scripture
in the past tense

i sit on a wooden bench
in a confessional built
by my grandfather
and other men
that fought wars,
knew the taste of truth
from the breath of
burning limbs

a young priest
listens to my fumbles
of speech
he checks his watch
remembers
Rebecca Teasdale
from *South Haven High*
the sway of her ass through a cotton skirt

guys like me fucked
girls like *Rebecca Teasdale*
and guys like the young priest
sat locked behind
bedroom doors
working their cock
and praying
Jesus to forgive
their sins

i walk past an old stone house
smoke lifts
from a chimney
spins between
branches
of a leafless tree

at the courthouse i turn
pause
wonder
what destination
i might take
as i trudge
past a statue of *Washington*
on a white stallion

he hasn't done
much
lately

either

a poem to a starving man

early sunrise gray sky morning
tramping down 6th Avenue
in the heart of hearts
downtown Los Angeles

i see him

dead eyes rheumy soul sifting
through debris overturned trashcan
rummaging digging searching
a beating heart searching

i see him

people pass pay no mind
no attention no words no solace
no comfort no peace no promise
no mind to see or feel or touch
they move and move and move
without eyes to see

i see him

he packs his cart filled with life
his life little things little memories
his life filled a shopping cart piled
with blankets and tin cans and little bits
of this and that his world his time
alone and lost and starving

i see him

he makes his way up the street up
to the corner up to the next direction
the next turn up to a passage never
up always down always down

i see him

he fades from view pushing his cart
his life alacrity wheels turning wobbling
stomach growling quiet starving
i stand frozen in place i move to follow
i move to change i move to offer
but feet stay frozen my motion zero
i move to follow but he is gone
and gone and i've done nothing
again nothing frozen not moving

i see him

which is almost worse than
not seeing him at all

brother stand up

brother stand up
face front
move ahead
inch after inch
after miserable fucking inch

we stand together
white black brown
queued and waiting
inch after inch...
waiting for the mission
to open doors to open
promise to open but we just move
(inch after inch...after)

words never fall from
our blistered lips our tired limbs hold just
enough to move us ahead move us forward
we yearn and want and beg
but nothing nothing nothing
this inch a mile this mile forever

the doors crack open
we take our paper plates
our plastic spoons
thankful for the meal
thankful for the rest
thankful for a moment
to be closer to human

brother stand up
rise up - tear at these
bleeding walls
brother stand up
change is coming
change is coming

or so they say
but when
the lights go down
we go back
stand in line
inch by inch
by miserable fucking
we stand in line

waiting

perfect biting teeth

he had a monogram on his shirtsleeve
perfect biting teeth
tan skin
he never fought a battle
but pointed so we'd know
which way to go

he took tips from
Hitler in the art of
compassion
littered courtyards
with skulls of the dead

i watched him cower
in shadows when someone yelled fire
when someone yelled free
he was first in line

he had a monogram on his gravestone
no one really bothered
i went out of curiosity
and free food at the wake

the downtown café

Saul and i met downtown
at a café on the corner
of 6th and *Los Angeles Street*
a no-name decrepit place
where vagrants and
transients linger
for cheap coffee
and a glimpse of the
smooth - shaven
leg of a fucked-out
9 to 5 waitress named *Betty*

> nice tits, a simple ass –
> PhD in romance languages from *Yale* –
> a bankroll provided in trust by a dead father –
> an ex husband rots under the patio
> of a little house in *San Pedro*
> bought and paid for with stolen doubloons -
> a crooked smile borrowed from too many lies –
> a fly paper tongue that never swallows –
> and a heart broken by a carpenter's hammer

Saul and i talk about
nothing - it's always nothing
as if we couldn't keep a conversation about
something going for more than a minute or two –

but i like *Saul*
because he doesn't
complain too much

or a tom waits love song

addiction comes
in different shades
and hues -
different strokes
of a brush
paint vistas
that don't always
make it to the
ten o'clock news
or into a tom waits
love song -

still the shame
we bury - our own -
lay deep in closets
made of muslin
and saffron
behind tidy boxes
and memories
etched on plate glass
windows -

we hide our fear
in other mendacities
other paradigms
other essentialities -

i hide mine
in sorrow
from a well
that never runs dry –

pawnshop

there's no swagger in my walk
as i make my way
down *Los Angeles Street*

i peer in a pawnshop
and delight that my broken
dreams are shared
by others

this specific place is
filled with shiny metal
and piecemeal memories -
all for a price well below cost

more than once i've traded my
past for beads and cholera blankets

the proprietor -
a tiny man with a sad smile
and broken teeth -
waves and buzzes me in

i trade my
rent for
someone's
odd heirloom –

and i think
maybe this
will roll
better with me

sister surrender

back alley winding street
tent city castles line
asphalt rivers
a past cut to our
graying faces
linoleum eyes bleed for focus

a young woman buries
her baby in tattered linen
buried in corners of a rich man's eye
forgotten by midnight
of a *December* day
she places her baby
on the steps of
St. Anthony's
stands out of sight
until the door shows *Jesus*
runs until her feet no
longer remember
cries until well runs dry

i see her feel her
want to scream
not to surrender
not to pass down
or pass out or
swallow the poison
but the cops find her
first dead in the
corner of a rich man's eye
the pipe still warm
but radiant memory dried to dust

morning fog lifts slow
on a slight breeze
cold lays flat on
faded concrete
croaking voices of morning
break through the light -
i touch soft the first
kiss of the sun

an old man in rags lay
curled deep in the folds
of his ratted-matted life
a hungry in his stomach -
lifeless in his eyes
i turn away - shame deep
in my molting skin

he smiles blankly at me
tired eyes rheumy with blight
a neglectful past/present/future
he smiles blankly at me

i offer the remains of my
breakfast to him - my hands
tremble with guilt

he is grateful but the meal
is cold - half eaten - barely
edible and i pause

at the door of the diner
i lead him in - we sit at the
counter - talk of past/present/future
others look away - a manager
protests but my mean eyes
push them away

homeless man eats heartily -
thanking me
at every other bite,
smiling true through
broken teeth and dirty lips
he offers memories - odd stories
old tales of a war - fighting
to save *American* lives - ten inches
of mud in *Vietnam*

'i never served,' i said

'we all serve, one way or another'

he cleaned his plate and one more
and went on his way

cars go by

the other day
i saw an old man
with a long gray beard
and soulful eyes
sitting atop a milk crate
up against a wall
just outside a liquor store

he appeared very
beatific
just sitting there
watching
cars go by

i went by, too

a couple of hours
later - done
with an odd list
of errands
and appointments
i drove back by

he sat there - still

i pulled into
a parking lot behind
a liquor store
and sat next to him
with my own milk
crate i found next
to a beat down dumpster

we sat there
he and i
without saying a word

as if this happened
to him
every day

gray clouds slowly gathered
and night pushed away
at the sun

the old man with
the gray beard and
the soulful eyes
stood
and looked at me
- through me
as if in a dream

he smiled and said
thank you
then disappeared

i drove that way
a time or two
but never saw him
again

although - on occasion
i will grab a milk crate
and sit
and
watch cars go by

rivers

when roman candles burn through city skies,
   i will flow through *Los Angeles*
the snapping turtles bite at turn signals
   i will flow through *Los Angeles*
with songs of no tomorrow sound
   i will flow through *Los Angeles*
and devils tell stories like nursery rhymes
   i will flow through *Los Angeles*
when red sparrows drop from yellow leafed trees,
   i will flow through *Los Angeles*
and silver snap car crash silhouettes shine
   i will flow through *Los Angeles*
trees weave in concrete towers
   and i will flow through *Los Angeles*
concrete cascades list against fallen angels
   i will flow through *Los Angeles*
with dreams of purple iris
   i will flow through *Los Angeles*
down on 6th when I dance
   i will flow through *Los Angeles*
where bobbing lizards are all the rage
   i will flow through *Los Angeles*
and smell the first breath of light
   i will flow through *Los Angeles*
my soil like ants in *December*
   i will flow through *Los Angeles*
and smile at transistor radios
   i will flow through *Los Angeles*

just as she flows through me

while in the country
i walked past a meadow
where a sheep herder joyfully
sodomized an ewe with a mangy
coat and glassy eyes

it reminded me of the government
and their position on the poor
not that the poor have mangy coats
or glassy eyes

although a friend of mine who lives
on skid row up in *Los Angeles*
has a glass eye and his coat
has seen better times - he
knows when to run when the
government comes around

tired Sunday

tired *Sunday* on the dime
down at the mission with
my plastic plate and spoon

we sit in rows like tiny soldiers
wait in silence as mourners
prepare coffins
filled with beans and franks

i tap *Morse* code through
dirty fingertips - songs
only other parishioners
of the street might know

rays of light build holograms
of invisible tomorrows -
reflections in various shades
of pink and gray - i raise my
hand as if to ask a question
but realize silently
i have nothing to say

a woman in church in a tight linen dress

a woman in church in a tight linen dress
sits draped in stain glass sunlight
smiling

it's *Sunday*
cold and i find comfort only
in the warmth of the place
not the voice from the pulpit

she looks at me with a sheltered stare
brown hair falling - curtains before her eyes
words form on ruby stained lips
but the crying demagogue
forces her astray

parishioners stand to sing, praise thee and what not
i remain seated - the curve of her ass
my temple

she moves three steps to her right
nearer to thee - i smell arcadia and a jasmine sky

they pass the plate, i take a loan
her eyes widen, her laugh so sweet

we walk to a coffee shop
i pay with *Jesus*-dollars

she sits at the edge of a silken bed
legs spread and waiting
i kneel before her, it's my turn to praise

scandal

back row sitting
at a local
network church
searching
more for warmth
than salvation
minister gets his groove on
a mesmerizing dance
of vowels, nouns
and bullshit

i listen a bit
as i eyeball
a young woman
in a tight dress
my stink
is no match
for her cologne

minister
stops
sudden

a tear in his eye
real for a change
the church had lost
every dime
of their savings
in some *Wall Street*
scandal

it must hurt
more when the
liars and cheats
lose it all

the plate
comes around
and i empty
my pockets
all my coins
bills
and lint

i already
taste the pain
of knowing
it comes free
and without
charge
there's nothing
i need
that i can't
steal,
beg
or borrow

but for
the minister
only cash
will help him
take off the
edge

last rites

no water
in a crystalline vase
and the flowers
are now dead
dust gathers in every corner

mail stacks up
against a pauper's door
bills and
advertisements
communication from
the outside world

no one knocks
rent not yet due
his family
long since moved away

lonely street
filled with
gray and
black
sometimes
when the sun finally shines
there's a taste of red

dishes stack in the sink
empty food cartons
slope around speckled tile
flies gather
leave maggot young
slithering on a plate

blood's congealed
gathered
blackened and dried

the stink of his rotting flesh
does not defeat
a hanging stink of
every day life

he left his papers
and books
on the step of a *Catholic Church*
a letter of apology
addressed
to god
and his team

no one reads the words
everything ends up in the church sale bin
out on the curb with
the other remains of broken lives

based on

i live in a tree atop high limbs
away from ivy

that grows from booted steps
and narrow lanes seldom passed.

an old car cries from window sills
chased by dragons

in pink satin teddies that speak in tones
of ancient *Chinese*.

sparrows build nests next to where i lay
at night dreaming.

there are moments when simple clarity
reminds me to

take the trash to the curb before it's
rescue becomes too well known.

i linger with thorns that form a rock cradle,
listen to a breeze

that echoes a mother's lullaby deep
in this garden.

koi nestle between boulders as reflections
remember trees

there is nothing here, but time and a shining
light that won't fade.

i stand corrected

there's a bar at the end of a road
that's marked with a 'one way, no exit sign'

how appropriate

it's a low-light, low-life
scum-of-the-earth,
whores-giving-head-in-
the-bathroom kind of place

my place
a friendly place
where no one knows my name
and no one gives a fuck
ever

drink, get drunk
move on

i'm sucking back cheap whiskey
shot by shot
counting time
and placing bets
on the time and day death
pulls my tag

when this woman with fuck me eyes
a wonder bra and six inch heels
walks in close and sits
up tight
at the bar

i taste her lips
drink her eyes
my imagination a cacophony of
indelicate poses

i buy her a drink
and toast her cleavage

when i ask her name
she says names aren't important
and i think, this is a good sign

i can see the sirens
up on the rocks
calling my name with
that sad same song
closer and closer
until the heat reaches from
the tips of her fingers up
to the base of my cock

there's no time for formalities
in the backseat of a cab
i make my peace with the sway
of her ass and follow her up
the walk, into her soul

buried forever there
and gasping for air

empty houses

fires burn down empty houses
as i walk down streets vacant of life,
only ghosts linger in the cool shade
of oleander and palm trees

i remember so well the words of my father
but i can no longer walk in his footsteps,
the path he knows goes much farther
than my heart will know to follow

thick black smoke burns my eyes
i find comfort on the back step of an old memory
an odd compendium of time and remorse
stacked like bibles in a downtrodden church

the devil dances with matches
striking them one by one
i watch the tips spark to life
before he flicks them onto un-
suspecting souls

at the end of another asphalt river
i step from the curb, neighborhoods awash
with blazing light, his eye meet mine
i know the shame of living, the sorrow of survival

i taste the ash upon my wicked tongue
mute from words stolen across dark ages
lost in memories of misdirection
my feet shuffle along
the sound scraping against my skin

the warmth of burning fresh upon my soul

fish harbor

i remember the clang of halyards cry
well before dawn

long thin bows cut silver grass
sending tides of rise and fall

a longing moan of inner harbor
buoy greets them as they go, off to
chase a crimson sun
gulls in their wake as they slowly gather speed

lights dim fade exhaust as angry pistons kick
with soulful force

i can hear the men move about
on black wood decks
laugh and drink coffee,
go about their day

we settle back to slumber, she and i,
three hours before
a mid-week rise
no other sound, or sight or thought
crosses through my mind, other
than the gentle creak
of a world spinning
'round

terms of parole

on the front step i sit watching children play
with sticks and rocks because *Christmas* is
a fantasy and something they cannot touch

and yet they laugh, cry out with joy, a sound
as alien as a twenty dollar bill left swimming in
a gutter with old cigarette butts

when the postman brings my catalogs and
electric bill, he points to a gutter and asks
if that's mine, i say sure, i flick my
spent butts there all the time, then he says no
that twenty dollar bill

i iron the bill flat and dry, buy plastic toys
at *Lee's Liquor Store*, the kind made in *China*
and brought over in gigantic metal cargo
containers in the guts of fat ships and give
them to the children on my step

their eyes flash in delight
as their give up their sticks and rocks

they play madly, loudly without remorse or question
and i sit smoking, waiting to be beamed up to heaven

or put back into jail

footsteps lay atop
dust covered floorboards of white oak and ash
mid century style furniture
covered with old stained linens

moth eaten window shades
hang limp and forgotten
mirrors fogged with timeless breath
of a distant age line the hall
next to cracked and yellowed
photographs of people no one remembers

doors creak as I pass over thresholds
the day, bright and fearless, slides between cracks

my heart races

trees restless, move to a silent rhythm
forest alive, we are surrounded
deep within

stillness fills me, i sit on the top step
memories flood over me
and rewrite the past

a little girl, no older than seven
plays too close to a boarded up well

a brother,
a best friend,
a hero against all demons
a year older, maybe two
watches in horror
as a loud crack sounds
the rush of air
of falling

and screaming
and screaming
and screaming

she appears before me locked in that age
that time:

all these years
still with me
all these memories
still with me
her smile
still with me
her heart
still with me

different souls dance on oak and ash
music fills my ears, a collective of recollections
gathered, this place explodes
the beatitudes of a thousand partitions
joined,

I am with her
    at last
all these years
    at last
with her
still with her
here in this place
    at last

traveling highway

i remember driving down
long stretches of vacant memories
past places where cockroaches
and alligators laid in wait, and waiting
for *Spanish* moss to burn from
structured buildings, near a graveyard
where my grandmother lay in rest

long foggy mornings felt soft, pressed
flowers in a phone book or bible, gentle
perfume of lilacs drift without intention
or ill will, float toward a pious sky
and a noble moon

poverty houses painted in different shades
of authority approved pastels with picket fences,
tall trees, and little children coughing
up their futures while parents eat discarded
remains of fallen soldiers and pop stars,
and dictator candidates inching toward
the fall

i remember my father, fat lips smoking,
brown hands telling stories about
pictures in a book stolen
from libraries or classrooms,
pictures in a book formless in my mind, bouncing
down single lane highways, past little
houses and schoolyards, past sanctuary
and salvation, straight into the heart
of hell itself

speed

speed doesn't do
everything
i had hoped it would

it doesn't
pay the bills
or mop the floor

or bring me flowers
when i vomit
on the couch

it makes my dick
susceptible
to changing weather conditions
what good is fucking
if you can't make it
to the end

out the gate
i knew
the need would build
would become more
become more
become more
but i'm not there

yet

speed
makes my mind nimble
makes me breathe
as if content
before i fuck away
tomorrow

you know
she is a whore
when she fucks
you
just for money

and days may become
night
become day before another
and i risk it all
when i test
another bump

but i'm no slave
and too scared
to become true reckless

yet i will continue
to adore her

at least for now
at this moment
this day
we are still friends

the dust of a hundred miles

i'll never be an astronaut
i am more like an archeologist
solitude of nightingales
a comfort i prefer

trees outside my window
make reference to peaceful dreaming
doctors sign prescriptions
soccer moms get high

a girl named *Amber Willing*
lives silent determination
she works on every corner
from six am 'til half past noon

i play in stone edged gardens
with crackheads and vagrant stoners
i struggle with amphetamine
it's a dance i'll never stop

we work though kinks and phrases
burned out alabaster
cut corners to find salvation
with every passing light

Joey knows the answer
Old Otis on the back lot
he has a reputation
a somber kind of skill

we steal from Sunday morning
crumpled bills in our pockets
we pay through secret signals
breathe in an amber day

i'll never dance with *St. Peter*
there's a tweaker in the corner
he's slamming to a back beat
some day that might be me

for now i'm just a scholar
so far from starting over
i passed all my finals
a hero on the rise

i found a home in gray fog
up near *Easter Island*
we lay in fields of rusting
tin cans and copper pennies

don't look at me in wonder
my station is to be frozen
in my head i'll still be dreaming
in truth i'm but a clown

digging ditches in *Australia*
writing poems in arboretums
i know i am an addict
it's not my only vice

bitter circus

short skirt, black heels, a voice an octave too low -
her head hangs down in a drink that never empties

ah, the bitter circus, back in town,
she's at center ring, fighting for attention

faces never linger, pause or offer simple explanation -
they reflect, biometric calculations, tasks of survival -
a means to an inglorious end

we speak in fragments, lost amidst ruins, reclamation for the
rich while the poor suck up dust

heat rises through a scarlet foundations,
whip snap anecdotes on a welfare check -
she twitches slightly,
Morse code dot and dash signs of life

love bleeds black in a starving belly -
her eyes glazed over, drinking with the dead
for now she is alive

i say hello in a muted salutation,
she smiles thin and bleak
knowing the offer about to come

we find darkness in a stall of a public restroom,
i fuck her without passion, it only makes breathing worse

she hangs her head low, another drink,
never ending, we part without comfort -
alone again and not transformed

road work

i've had a hundred jobs and
i'll have a hundred more
before they put away
the spears
and call this war a draw

angels will still linger
on doormats of disrepair
alive in knowing
that respectable people
still step light

the last time i went
to the corner market
two *Mexican* kids
were arguing about baseball
and the proprietor - a
man from *Istanbul* -
just shook his head

i answered an ad from
the weekly flier - ten days
work digging ditches
along a road out
in the *Mojave*
it's pays a hundred bucks
a day and i thought -
why not

solitary confinement

these crimes -
my own
committed
in fair light
brought down shackles
and an eight by eight
cell

three paces up -
three back
a sick slap -
 slap step
through a skyless night
through screams across metal walls

i kept pushing -
words and lies
endless thoughts
from a *Caspian* pen
littering sidewalks
with dismembered
allegory and rhetoric

simple really -
a chance to climb
to ride across *Ikaros'* sun
yet fate coils around delicate blood
leaves me clinging
motionless
burned flesh
charred and falling away

death starts
at the first breath drawn
gains momentum
as find that first peak

drawn to your challenge -
beating against electric light
not knowing to stop
when my skull gets smashed in

guard calls lights out -
i take up my queue
three paces up
three back
a sick slap, slap step
through a skyless night
through screams across metal walls

changing places

when i turned 12
my family moved
down to *Orange County, CA*
where houses look like movies
and soccer moms never grow old

my mother bought my birthday cake
at the local grocery store for the first time

i didn't realize then
the change that
had taken place

within a few years i fell in with the
moral majority in the midst of redemption at the
Covenant's shiny church

we took sides during the growing pandemic
of *Christ's* salvation while communing with saints
of *Wall Street* and *Madison Avenue*

you see, i had no choice in this modern behavior
programmed like a postage stamp
deep in fascination just as ink begins to dry

it took 30 years to find safe harbor
and salvage my beggar's rice

when i see birthday cake at a grocery store

i cringe

and hope memory
never fades

sideshow jack

when i was a kid
i wanted to run away
with the circus
work with the freaks
and carnies

i would have fit in

now i find
that i actually
did join -
a circus of
lemmings
two shows
a night
played
out in three rings

laughter, at me,
not with me
sparks my
imagination

when i was
a kid
i should
have dreamt of
hell

it would have
worked out
better than this

freshly minted and released early for good behavior

the holy ghost and i have a lot in common
not really, but it's a good lie to start with

a tall skinny black kid came to the door today
selling magazines and books so he could go to college
maybe i shouldn't mention color
when you read the word *black* you already reached
a conclusion

tall kid in nice clothes and enough charm
to sell the *Passion of Christ* full mark up to *Moses*
knocked on my door today
usually i say *no thank you* ten or so times before realization
hits, before the magazine seller slumps
stutters away

today i stood there and
i saw myself
and
i spoke to myself
and
i asked myself
could i knock on a door selling magazines
and books so i could go to college

i thought, no

in my right hand i held a notice,
a loan repayment schedule, from *Obama*

Obama sent me a postcard from *Turkey*
weather's fine, wish you were here
i was there but the restraining order keeps
me five hundred yards away

the kid goes into his pitch, it's not bad, i've heard them all
he smiles a little too much, i tell him this, he thanks me
seems like a small price to pay

when i get the details i'm genuinely interested that he get
through school
suddenly it's very important,
more important than
anything else

i make a couple of calls
Obama doesn't pick up, i text him
out of office
Bush II picks up on the first ring,
he's home most days in *Crawford*
doesn't have much to say
never did, really

this kid's got a dream, real or otherwise
feels real, genuine at least
a degree in marketing
run an *Automotive Aftermarket* shop
'you know sir?
cool rims, badass stereo, lights on the under carriage'

he's paying for school the hard way
door to door, pitching magazines and books
to people like me
home in the middle of the day
writing an academic paper no one will read
preparing for a presentation no one will have interest in
receiving a degree that is ... (comment deleted by censor)
sudden note from *Obama*:
met with the Turkish leaders, they seem nice
had a great cup of coffee,
took a nap on
Air Force One

a better move, set up a scholarship,
or something,
one less kid banging on doors,
waking me from my dull sleep,
selling magazines and books to wary citizens
out of work and at home in the middle of the day

my mirror knows my selfish heart
my greed and ego
i really don't think that way

the kid and i chatted for twenty minutes
i bought two books, had it donated
to a hospital in *Kenya* or *St. Louis*
maybe fate will pay me back
doesn't matter, his smile seemed enough

Obama responds, again, to my text
it took a couple of hours
said he enjoyed the new *Star Trek* movie
i texted back: *i did too*

that screaming you hear is mine

the worst lie
is the one you tell yourself
one that offers hope
and
a glimpse of a normative future

the lie you whisper
into the mirror each morning
before you trudge off
to another day of wasted time
another day chasing realities
well beyond the grasp
of your yearning fingers

for two years
i reached out
and
nearly felt
the warmth of a promise that offered an out
from the mendacity
of this modern life
an escape
from the global village of suburban bliss

it became the proverbial carrot
a perfect cunt
a perfect smile
free dope open to all
a selfish dream
where i could become something more
than this broke down 45 year old sack of rotting flesh
a third rate poet in a second rate town
laying in a box under neon
sucking cock for another line,
another lie
another ten minute escape

don't tell me it's pity
don't look down at me from the
tip of your spiky nose
don't try to put your feet
into my thrift store shoes
i did everything right,
followed the checklist
paid fees
dues
the journal
the press
the radio show
the tutoring,
the academic papers
the mindless lectures
seminars to salvation

all for what? to feed the lie...

i remember
the day
when i received the note
on thick rich paper
the note that said
you are in
you are a part of the club
another team
another delusion
even then i knew
but i buried my head
deep in my own ass
this rainbow has an end
there is a song
in here
somewhere

but they don't prepare you for reality
they don't prepare you
for the "*Irish Need Not Apply*" signs
on the academic halls
they don't tell you that the paper you paid for
is worth little more
than the one you wipe your ass with,
of course, this paper, this single sheet,
you'll pay for the rest of your life

too bad i didn't read him
two years ago and realize
paths are not permanent
but like a stupid moth
i draw to electric light
smash myself against it
again and again and again
until the life ghosts from my flesh
and i fall to concrete
awaiting
the final foot

to stomp my last breath

and we've still a ways to go

i stand near the edge
of a million faces strong,
stare at yearning people
as they smile bright

for one shining moment
they raise their hands,
their voices,
as a pre-recorded
quartet plays a lullaby

'this is it', they say
'the moment is now'
'change is here'
then they turn in the cold
walk back home waving plastic
American flags made in China,

sit in front of their TV
and wordlessly watch

another factory closed
another family red tagged
another child buried in a crowded classroom
another student turned away from hope

and i remember that word
hope
i remember the sound
as in ping-ponged
across radio waves,
from east to west
north to south

hope – hope - hope

another bank goes under
another mall is shuttered
another family gets evicted
another mother loses healthcare
i keep waiting for voices to rise
voices other than blue and red
- finger pointing
- veins bulging
- teeth dripping
i hear those voices
those school ground maniacs
as they fight for control of the tetherball,
in *Congress, Sacramento*

if you ask me,

i'd layoff the lot
put them in line
on a freeway off ramp
with dirty cup and gritty smile
put them in a welfare queue
the hiring office
the dying office

take their houses and cars and pinstriped suits,
their perfect smiles and $400 dollar haircuts,
take their healthcare and 401K

put all the politicians
all the big business bobbleheads
CEOs
mortgage lenders
Big Three Automotive Executives

and put them in the lettuce fields
down in *Arizona* next to an immigrant's fence
let them survive on $80 a day,
stooped and bent, fingers gnarled arthritic

***

so where are the other voices

the lady at *Walmart* that has two jobs
the man who lost his home even though he
bought it the right way
the family that lives
   in a blue van at the end of my street
the girl that turns tricks
   behind the seven-eleven
   because she never knew better

teachers, semi-skilled laborers, retail workers
busboys, clerks, state workers

where are you? where's your voice?

where's the scream of the beat down, forgotten?
those near dead, and rotting?

when i close my eyes
all i can see are the images of the WPA
   1930s
dustbowls and field camps and bank runs
and long flat highways to *California*

i turn off my TV
check email
   289 applications
   no response
Master's Degree, Bachelor's Degree
doesn't mean a thing
not now not today
my twitching hand grabs a pen
i wonder where is my scream
where is my voice?

and i realize

it's right here
it's a start,
in syllable and sound
uptown words
and downtown truth

even as the flatulence of the pen
sours the air of my room
i realize,

we've still a ways to go

Darby Crash never sang like he was from New York City

it is 1:15 PM, a *Friday*, in *Los Angeles*,
well, near *Los Angeles*,
in the quiet space
before *Easter* and all the ruckus that will cause -

it's 2009
and i call my dealer
to make a purchase
but it seems he is on holiday or something
i change the song on my *iPod*
there's too much traffic
on the freeway
and there's a cop next to me
so i can't make a phone call
(it's illegal now)
and i really don't know the people that will deal to me

i pull off the freeway in
East Las Angeles,
up near the college
i will not teach at,
and order tacos from a catering truck
que ella es hermosa, incluso con grandes dientes
smog fills the skyline
and tall buildings hide
at the *ATM* my account coughs up zeros
the insecticide from the gardeners spray makes me dizzy

on *Los Angeles Street*
brown skin toy sellers
make offers
dos por uno, sólo cinco dólares
and i buy little things,
ray guns and baby dolls,
for my nieces and nephews

they like bright pinks and blues,
sometimes yellows,
but generally not orange or red

back in my car i drive past
the *Knitting Factory*
remember the first day
he and i met, hung out,
traded jokes, shared our dope,
he went out on stage
i stood in a trance as sound whispered like
a 707 in my ear

next day at *Denny's*, over on *Sunset*
not on *La Cienega Blvd.*,
the talking head
made an announcement
on analog televisions set
and i thought
of something different

and realized everything changed

December begins winter

i remember the sound of your voice
and the laughter of your eyes.

you stood at the end of an old
wooden pier and i suddenly realized,

everything.

your incantations of life melt
across snow and i watch

strange birds lift away
from treetops.

your world exists under canopies of gray,
never to change or borrow from
rainbow palettes. can it be that
the cloth we thought we both
found shape upon really exists

as a quilt from different beginnings?
something sewn tightly together by helpful hands?

i know the answer and you do as well,
but there on the old wooden pier
your feet stay in place, they do not move,
they do not surrender.

we both know where this ends. how the
last page will read. so many chapters
to go. i am a slow reader and you like
to skip ahead.

devoid of life, except for her

she tells me she loves me without using words
or language that can be written -
her eyes remind me of weekends
harbors at first light
Christmas in the country
small towns covered in perfect snow

there are moments as strangers evolve into lovers
and as lovers we find solace sheltered
beneath cotton covers

and a clanging brass chime
reminds of wind in treetops
a tree too willful and proud to bend,
too eager to stand tall and deny
the breath of a bitter god -

some say we are children
before the eyes of a higher voice -
i disagree -
we are merely forgetful and we fail to acknowledge
that which we made to understand things
we cannot -
too many have given up reason and prefer to be led -

she smiles when i say things like this,
when i philosophize in my matter-of-fact voice,
the one i borrow when i stand atop a crate
and speak to a street devoid of all life
except for her

last week I landed in India

New Delhi
it's a bit overwhelming
LA traffic without the cars

University invited me
to read poetry
teach a couple
of classes
the letter held a plane ticket
and a check that didn't bounce

so i went

i had to get a passport
and a *Visa*
and a series of shots
no one told me the shots were optional
i still got them
i'm ignorant that way

India is loud
a thousand children
at *Christmas*
crammed into a small room
opening presents
at the same time
kind of loud
maybe louder

people everywhere stare at me
i'm the foreigner

an extravagant woman
with giant eyes
impressive breasts
and an ass i'd follow anywhere

greets me at the gate
helps me with my bag
takes me to the hotel
joins me for dinner
fucks me on my bed
puts breakfast on her tab
showers without shame
laughs indecently
sits in the front row
takes notes during lecture
reads a poem about fucking
i realize it's about me

i feel old
like *India*
but some how
not as loud

i use a tool made of metal

1.   i use a tool made of metal
        to turn wet brown dirt.
        a gray duck
        with a turkey smile
        snaps at thin worms
        as they run,
        before they dig
        sightlessly
        into
        soil.

2.   the sun is warm.
        i am sitting
        on the back step.
        Dexter sits impatient
        on my lap.
        he is a gray cat.
        he reminds me
        of an aging porn star
        at an uptown dinner party.

3.   the duck digs.
        worms run.
        a snapping turtle
        sits on a white rock.
        the koi slow their circles.
        it is almost noon.
        i am writing
        when
        i should be reading.
        poetry no longer interests me.

4.   my girlfriend is out.
        airplanes land
        on a dirt strip
        near my house.

a female voice
calls for her dog.
i hear wind
in trees.
we are all dying.
some more quickly
than others.

5.   i received another rejection,
not from a potential employer
of course.
i am not as attractive
as most ,
as well as a poet,
so my training is complete.

coda: simply stated: my rejection.
i pay no respects, to the living or
the dead

who says that Romans can't dance
(when Helen's not around?)

1.   there's another poet i am reading,
       i do not like it -
       there's a spot on my liver, i saw it
       in an x-ray -
       there's so much whining, i think i
       am similar -

       is there catharsis in text or is my imagination
       forfeiting reality?

       i just tore the cover from a book of poetry
       that has a pink cover
       and ate it -
       i just vomited -
       the world forces me
       to admit things i do not
       want to -
       what is this obsession with my cock?
       structural assimilation is overrated -
       i don't want to be a poet,
       perhaps i should
       be a pirate -
       i keep checking email for a future
       but it's only
       spam and offers for generic *Viagra*

2.   something in me makes me crazy
       but it's not for your perusal -
       Mexican gardeners go through the motions -
       nothing is in the mail except bills and offers for
       generic *Viagra* -
       i tire so easily, perhaps i am dying -
       my stomach turns, it's that pink cover
       from that book of poetry

3.   i took a break but i am back -
        my step-daughter is laughing;
        it scares me -
        poetry has left me, maybe i left it -
        i have other things to do;
        make money, pay bills,
        get out of the house more often -
        it's almost summer and the trees are greening -
        i read more of that poetry book,
        the one without
        the pink cover and i threw it across the room -
        i won't return to it, i am done -
        maybe i will write a book that a reader
        might throw across a room or tear off the cover -
        i will have the cover laced with acid
        or heroin so eating it will have meaning
        or an affect other than vomiting although
        that may be uncontrollable
        but what am i talking about?
        didn't i mention i am done with this poetry thing?
        maybe i did -
        i don't recall and i do not enjoy re-reading -
        it'll have to be an assumption

5.   there's dead flowers in the kitchen,
        vase water changed colors -
        my partner says i am jealous -
        i ask about what,
        she says everything -
        i don't respond -
        on the corner of *Olive* and *Main* is an *AM/PM*,
        i purchased a *Slurpee* -
        this does not matter, hold meaning, etc -
        poetry like this makes me vomit,
        pink pages fill the toilet -
        academics seem to like it -
        well, some do

7.   it's three days later -
        4:28 AM in the morning -
        my little dog woke me with her scratching,
        if i bathe her i will drown her -
        i don't have to be up for three hours
        but i cannot sleep
        and it's not due to dope
        or intoxication,
        for a change -
        i burned
        the formerly pink covered book of poetry,
        it has proven a more complete resolution -
        all my other poetry books i
        list as used on Amazon -
        i don't think they will sell but
        it costs me nothing until i sell them -
        right now they are in a box,
        in the garage,
        labeled with a black sharpie -
        a time capsule -
        we did one in third grade,
        each class put something in it
        in *1972* -
        those were the last days of
        Vietnam
        and *Watergate*
        before *Resignation* and *Aaron's Home Run* -
        they opened it in *1997* but
        i had moved away and forgotten -

11.   my wireless connection is not working
        perhaps i should be hardwired,
        perhaps i should sleep more,
        but so much is changing -
        i moved the boxes around in
        the garage
        and took out the trash -

13.   three days later and i broke my promise,
        the one about never returning to a poem,
        especially so long
        after i started it, so long
        after i took measure, aim and fired,
        but here i am, three days later,
        annoyed more that my step-daughter
        drank almost all of my *Gentleman Jack*
        whiskey and remains convinced i
        am stupid enough to realize
        that i might forget to remember
        that maybe i did it and i didn't –

19.   i bought another copy
        of the pink book but this one has a cover
        or, i should say, had a cover – i tore this
        one off as well but didn't eat it –
        my mind melts a little more
        when i read it and i read it
        and i read it and i read it and i read it -
        the doctor says it's indigestion –
        the black spot turns out
        to be a hologram of something else –
        it's *Saturday* and i am not doing anything
        other than wandering on the page
        without any result or meaning –
        seems like i am repeating –

23.   it's three days later,
        nothing
        it's three days later,
        still nothing

29.   just motions, landing a plane on a foggy tarmac or
        fishing without a line or dreaming in black and white –
        maybe i should put more fish in the *aquarium* but
        that's a different sort of drama

six images somewhat unrelated

a television flickers between snow
  and rolling images as an old man
  fiddles with rabbit ears not
  realizing that analog signals have
  been discontinued for reasons
  of progress

a priest shoots dope in a confessional
  a nun puts her pale hand on an oak
  pew, sits in the back of her knees, holds
  a bible her mother gave her after the
  nun's first communion at 13, tears
  fresh on soft skin, lips tremble,
  words say,
  forgive me father for i have sinned

a man stands in front of a *Seven/Eleven*
  lighting a cigarette he found in an ashtray,
  scratching at a beard he cannot afford
  to shave, wearing pants that have not
  been washed in several months, standing
  in shoes that do not rest

a girl sits in a waiting room, her hand
  on her belly, fluorescent lights say
  more than the eyes of the protesters
  outside the clinic, a nurse passes
  by without judgment, another girl
  around the same age reads about
  Paris Hilton in *People Magazine*
  and sobs quietly and a boy nearly
  the same age chews his fingernails

a *President* stands at a window, stares into a rose
   garden, his arms are crossed, he is alone for
   the moment, but the *Prime Minister* from
   Pakistan is on line six and holding, the *Secretary
   of Defense* is waiting in the hall, a former *President*
   is fucking a social worker in his office in *Harlem*,
   a lobbyist from the Insurance industry folds
   unmarked bills into legislation

a man of middle age signs a contract for
   silver dollars, a bag of dope waits in a top drawer,
   atop a $100,000 check from the *First Bank of
   Please Bend Over*, he cuts a vein to
   sign the promise, he cuts a line to make it through

mirror, mirror

an actor sits backstage peeling away paint
  clown white skin
  smiling face
  a red nose

paint comes away easy
skin takes longer

when his lips melt away
the smile is permanent
his perfect teeth available for all to see

he tears off his scalp
begins in on the muscle and veins

each piece is portioned into perfect piles
segregated by category

it takes a few hours until he's finally
down to bone

just before midnight
gray rats scurry
across a darkened stage
he pieces himself back together
with super glue and scotch tape

past the mirror there are no changes
but in his hand a knife
always finds the truth

if success is revenge then i failed at that too

being sober is relative
you know? in this part of town
L.A.
a tired old bitch
with more to say than
i want to hear

so, yeah, i got the notice
time's up
pay up
gov't pulled my paper
they know where i live

hey buddy can you spare a dime
to a fellow American down on his luck?

in the backyard there's a tree
that still reaches for the sky
every morning
when the sun wanders by
and i wonder...well, i don't really

they put me on the docket
the big event, my last event
30 minutes
45 if i want
to read
anything
anything, i ask
sure
really, i said, not as a question
more in disbelief
they hand me a list of rules
maybe ten minutes, i said
sure

Martin Luther
not *King*, the other one
nailed his note to an oak door
of a church
the *Pope's Church*
the *Holy Roman Catholic Church*
essentially saying:

go fuck yourself

i left my hammer at home
and they hid the tape and thumbtacks

at the dais
i stand a few minutes
drift off
my mind wanders
a bit

well,

you know?

right?

i could apologize

i could apologize
        but i won't
i could tell the truth
        but i need a nap
i could quit snorting speed
        but real time is too vague
i could pay for sex
        but there's no check in my mailbox
i could sing
        but my voice betrayed us all
i could find hope
        but every rock is overturned
i could promise
        but where would that get us?

i could resume my proper direction
        but, well, there's nothing clever here to say
i could dance
        but my feet are locked in stone
i could fly
        but my dealer's out of town
i could register at college
        but my tears hurt when i sneeze
i could laugh
        but that seems pointless
i could stand
        but my back has too many holes
i could write something brilliant
        but i never did before
i could leave
        but my home is a garbage can
i could whisper something delicate
        but my tongue is like a mule's
i could steal back those married years
        but where's the point in that?

i could live in the moment
        but this moment's a stain
i could go to rehab
        but i failed that once before
i could stop before i started
        but a fool never slows
i could believe in *Christianity*
        but my skin melts in the sun
i could dream
        but sleep is chemically alternated
i could do something better
        but my glass is empty now

false ambition, sudden end

i can't get it out of my head
at night
when i am supposed to be sleep dreaming
- cobwebs form on ceiling fans
- freeway buzz 12 blocks away
- trash trucks rumble past schoolyards
- train whistle's shriek simple truth

you see, i turned left when most went right
maybe they all went right
my phone no longer rings –
my lazy feet settle atop a new path
one covered in dirt and twigs,
fallen leaves,
one barely traveled -
i travel through alleys, clinics, backrooms, and taverns;
high deserts and low –
i fill out forms, sign my name
acquire debt as easily as i breathe

two years gone,
doors closed,
keys lost,
feet shackled
my skin peels from the bone under a phallus sun

my pockets fill with smooth stones and i step from
the end of a pier,
confident in my next destination
although i wouldn't be surprised
if that was a lie
as well

randomness is beguiling

i started the other day in a stupor
thinking about small things
the price of bread and gas and heroin
odds and sods of a daily life
mixed metaphors about freedom,
hope, and breathtaking splendor

my mind drifts, you see, from place to place
with relative ease and i often wonder
what spins behind your mind

after all, you are only a picture

i guess i am too

the day goes on and i fill my time with
a mix of nightmares and chores
i clean the garage, my office space,
six loads of laundry

in the end, it's *New Year's Day*
nothing special
not really
just going through the motions
like any other day

except

i have your picture
and intrigue and something new
to ponder

tiny spaces make me nervous

certain days
remind me
of *Bolivian* summers
dunes of sand
shifty
under lazy skies

Blackberry alarm clocks
break my pastoral beatitude
i eat milk-barren cereal
straight from a box
brittle bones snap
from cyanide intervention
there's no camera in the bag

words stack
next to a stone mason's bricks
i split the infinitive
and dot a forgotten i
buffaloes roam on torn out pages
memories litter
a pilgrim's highway
yesterday's tomorrow,
for some

there's a question i forgot to ask

so good it sells itself

some days i feel like an infomercial pitch man
selling some useless trinket everyone should own

i show you value six different ways, in color, with charts
my voice climbs and shrills, proclaims and shocks

one time offer, just like last week and tomorrow,
double the deal if you call in right now

kind of like congress or legislators in *Sacramento*
they pitch their product, point fingers at opposition

play games in the margins, tell lies from the front row,
lay in wait for weakness, assume there are empowered

by citizens in their districts
that really have no clue –

you see,
it's their way or no way, no communion in the aisle,
to me they are all devils and need to go back to hell

i listen to speeches, *Republican* responses, a little fat kid
named *Joey* tries to keep up

the *History Channel* shows a *World War II* documentary
and i remember how war ended the *Depression*

before i return to dreaming
i wonder where we'll be next year

exodus

(from a world that never existed except in metaphor and debtor's memory)

of course, they said, *hello*, they said and i rose like night over
the *Caspian* Sea
this is a line, dotted and all, sign with blue ink, won't you?

guaranteed submission upon admission
hobbled by the hammer of a long dead carpenter
blue eyes no longer respond to the reflection of light

i drove through red lights in *Middletown, Connecticut*
rain torrents, *Morse* code warning,
i remember then forgot
at the airport they searched my bags
then me but found nothing

Wm. Burroughs plays cards in café in *North Beach*
Sid died for all of my sins and some of yours
Henry Miller squints at the sway of a tight yellow dress
Kathy Acker plays with scissors atop *Anne Sexton's* grave

i read chapbooks in a bar next to *City Lights Bookstore*
gray fog fills cracks in a linoleum floor,
a man next to me asks a question,
even though i begin to speak i say nothing
he walks to the bathroom but never returns

the only things i know are things that i've borrowed
a consummate liar, a cheat on the throne
television commercials broadcast messages encoded
i left my pen at the pulpit and wandered away

fuck is just a word until you walk into the room

a friend sits
on an old creaking barstool

> *yes, this poem starts in a bar*
> *and ends up here*

where was i, just then?
i forgot
oh wait, i remember now

a friend sits
on an old creaking barstool
drinks room temperature beer
from a borrowed glass
days hold no significance
a barrister's clock stuck at three
ticks without movement
and i smile

there are no outlaws, he said
no underground, really
just because you write fuck in a poem
doesn't make you interesting, he said

a *Chinese* porter from the *Biltmore
Hotel* orders coffee to-go
and says polite things
like please and thank you
he glances at a television screen
the score remains 3 to 1

you live in the past, i said
a dream, almost, a fallen tree
you don't live at all, my friend said
a Martian landscape devoid of life
except for blinking robots rolling around

an illegal alien mops the floor
with dirty water
i can smell piss, shit and stale beer
in the air
jukebox plays a *Bobby Darin* song
a siren sounds outside the door

there's a story in all of us, my friend said
that's a myth and you know it, i said
i got a job at Home Depot, my friend said
i said nothing in response

disco postcard

i never worry about tense
as in *present, past, future* -
grammar is about structure
and politics and the price
of exported rice to *Costa Rica* -

in *1985* i spent the summer
in *Vietnam*, before *American*
and *Japanese* Corporations
built factories and returned
the population to imprisonment
and shameless propaganda -

i lived in the countryside
on a forged *Canadian* passport
a sketchy 6 month visa
based on cultural exchange -
no one in the village seemed
to bother with my presence -
they had bigger issues with
water buffalo and heat waves -

a 24 year old female *Belgian* junkie
smoked opium and bribed officials -
exported a variety of illegal
items through *Laos* and *Cambodia*
and slept under my mosquito tent
when rainless lightning struck
across treetops -

when the screaming stops you
can hear the diesel engines of
government trucks choke up dirt paths -

we hid in the underbrush of insanity -

Communist officials arrested the *Belgian* junkie –
deport her back to *Brussels* -
i got a official notice in the mail -
i returned to *Ho Chi Minh City* with
hopes of *Bangkok* or *Barbados* -
i ended up in *Phoenix* with nothing left
but time -

i received a disco postcard -
return address: *Antwerp Prison* -
a microdot of acid makes
the lemmings go away -

periphery

1. in the beginning

in the brightest noon sun shadows still linger
atop a concrete so hot it will burn your feet
should you forget to keep moving and suddenly
stand all alone

2. observations from the corner of the ring just before the bell

i watch a tall man
with innocent shoes
and a silver beard
walk into a corner
liquor store -
his sorrow bends
into the wilting folds
of his sagging age
and i wonder why
skies still swallow
clouds as little birds
stand on barbed wire

there's no solace in
silence, a chamber
snaps tight
and i look in
different direction -
a church burns
at the end
of a street
and the cries
of dominion
lift across
a northerly breeze -
firemen brandish
waterfalls -

hissing snakes
stream across
the black river -

3. a reason conversation suddenly ends

at 1:45 am on a
Friday night
i saw two
men burn to death,
trapped inside
a *Datsun 510* on
the side of *I5*,
wrapped in tangles
of oleander -
you could
taste it
before you
saw it
and when you
saw it
you couldn't
look away -

i slowed and asked
if i could help in
any way and a tearful
man directing traffic
shook his head -

only god can help us now

and i thought
that's not quite true
but an argument would
serve no purpose
so i just drove home

*4. the difference between innocence and shame is as narrow as
the line between here and there*

a priest sits
at my table
without asking
and i close
my book -
he smiles,
compliments
the sunshine -
he does not
seem to notice
ash carelessly
floating

perhaps the nervous
twitch in his fingers,
or the burnt fringe on
the right sleeve
of his black coat, or
the halo of gray on
his collar
knows
the correct time

rolling gutterballs with brand Obama™

Mr. President, i have question
or maybe a comment,
or maybe a scream yet to be heard

i look around
wonder
with all this suffering
with all this anguish,
why only crickets keep chirping
why parents stuff their hands in deep pockets
why lawyers stay silent
why teachers start crying as if they've nothing to say
why construction workers don't take up arms
why bipartisanship is a lie

in times like these
you don't have 100 days,
there is no honeymoon,
either put up or get out,
brand *Obama*™
the country is crumbled,
destroyed at the center
from lack of parental supervision,
we let children take control,
the ones in gray suits and pinstripes,
the ones up on *Wall St*
yeah they fucked us first,
just like *Congress* fucks us now

donkeys and elephants
measure their dicks to prove domination
while little blond girls
sit in dirt forgotten
rotting from malnutrition
lack of love
lack of home

since we'll be socialist by *Sunday*,
(how else will we recover),
let's string em up
in the tall trees
along the reflecting pool
under the dead eyes
of *Washington* and *Lincoln*

brand *Obama*™
i read all about the stimulus package
from a newspaper
i found in a bus stop
as i sat waiting

today i can eat,
tomorrow i have shelter,
in six months
i will be homeless
- *hey mom! look at me now* –
the *Republican* street walkers want less taxes
for their conjugal lovers
big business and lobbyists,
those stinking whores from the right
and the *Democrats* are not faultless,
with their bleeding pork barrel addiction
if you can wrangle these ducks,
mr. president,
i will loan you my gun

yesterday i had a conversation
with a friend i no longer know
he is but a shadow, face drawn,
eyes filled with fear we all share
his job dangles precariously,
his house could be taken,
he eats one less meal
because the nest is still full –

it's funny how eyes open
suddenly see
- when its your stomach calling,
you realize you're not alone,
but the streets are filled
citizens of disenfranchisement,
they've known
recession all of their lives –
there's a third world country
on the black rivers
of *Los Angeles*,
like ghosts without focus,
they've always been around

brand *Obama*™ i wonder
if you remember your history,
the shadows of
memory found in a book –
children without families,
mothers without hope
down in the dustbowl
or on the road to the sea –
in the 1930s the *Okies* had *California*,
in 2009 where do we go?
brand *Obama*™ i don't blame you,
i know it's near impossible,
the cunt you replaced
nearly had us imprisoned,
but prison is inevitable
if we don't change the game

i stare at pictures,
ones laid before me,
i see in the eyes,
a truth of my own
through toil and suffering
somehow they made it,
our ancestors' grandparents,

our fathers and mothers,
yet we stand on ground substantially different,
how many of us could carry a plow?
or till the soil?
or build a fire without burning it all down?
we rely on machines to make baking soda,
we rely on *China* to build everything else
today we are lazy and greedy,
we've forgotten our history,
we've forgotten each other
look at us now

did we also forget
that war fed our hungry
built rooftops
bought clothes and nylons and TV
near nuclear obliteration, a cold war fanaticism
a delicate house now falling down

in change we grow stronger,
a future yet colored
my years chained to the pew
tells me
Armageddon starts now
and i won't drop to my knees
pray to a stranger,
salvation is internal
and found in the slap of my cheap shoes
on pavement

in the dust of the future
we will find transmigration,
i don't worry so much about tomorrow –
my trepidation lay in what we will find

NeoPoiesis
a new way of making

in ancient Greece, poiesis referred to the process of making
creation – production – organization – formation – causation
a process that can be physical and spiritual
biological and intellectual
artistic and technological
material and teleological
efficient and formal
a means of modifying the environment
and a method of organizing the self
the making of art and music and poetry
the fashioning of memory and history and philosophy
the construction of perception and expression and reality

NeoPoiesis Press
reflecting the creative drive and spirit
of the new electronic media environment

LaVergne, TN USA
24 September 2009
158963LV00001B/5/P